Beautifully Crafted in God's Image

"So God created mankind in his own image, in the image of God he created them..."
Genesis 1:27 (NIV)

Beautifully Crafted in God's Image

"So God created mankind in his own image, in the image of God he created them..."
Genesis 1:27 (NIV)

RUBY ROBINSON

URDestined Publishing LLC

Copyright © 2024 by **Ruby Robinson**

All rights reserved. No portion of this publication may be reproduced, distributed, or transmitted in any form or by any means, without the publisher's or author's prior written permission.

URDestined Publishing LLC

Middleburg, Florida 32068

urdestinedpublishing@aol.com

Unless otherwise indicated, Scripture quotations are EasyEnglish Bible (EASY) and King James Version (KJV).

Scripture quotations marked (NIV) are taken from the Holy Bible, New International Version (NIV). Copyright © 1973, 1978, 1984, 2011 by Biblica, Inc. Used by permission of Zondervan. All rights reserved worldwide. www.zondervan.com The "NIV" and "New International Version" are trademarks registered in the United States Patent and Trademark Office by Biblica, Inc.

Beautifully Crafted in God's Image

ISBN 979-8-9916406-0-2 (ebook)

ISBN 979-8-9916406-1-9 (Paperback)

Printed in the United States of America

Dedication

This book is dedicated to every woman who is battling breast cancer, survivors who have overcome the disease, those grieving the loss of loved ones to breast cancer, and supporters. I am praying for you. You continue to fight this fight so gracefully. To those of you who have won the war already, you are absolute warriors. To our family and friends who are and have been right there by our side during this journey, you are what makes getting through it possible. We are so grateful to have your love and support carrying us through the hardest of times.

Table of Contents

Preface viii

Prologue x

Stage 1 Why? 1

    Why 2

    A Mother's Dark Secret 3

    Oh, That Day 4

    Loss 5

    Just Thinking 7

    You Were There 8

Stage 2 Courage 9

    Courageous Sister 10

    That Word 11

    A Warrior's Courage 12

Stage 3 Hope 13

    Hope 14

    My Strength 15

    Symbolism of Shades of Pink 16

Stage 4 Never Give Up 17

    Never Give Up 18

    There is a CAN in Cancer 19

    Still Able 20

    Gift of Now 21

REMISSION 23

    Beautifully Crafted 24

Prayers	27
Scriptures	37
Acknowledgments	47
About the Author	49
Contribution by	50

Preface

Beautifully Crafted in God's Image: A spirit-led collection of works on Breast Cancer.

While the path has not been easy, through perseverance and faith all things are possible. My first experience with breast cancer in 2006 began a journey I was not yet ready for. Unaware that my mother silently battled the same illness in its final stages, it was not until medical intervention could no longer aid her that our family's truth came to light. In those difficult moments, I found solace in journaling and poetry, which became outlets that provided comfort and clarity. After achieving remission in 2007, none of us could foresee that fourteen years later fate would call me to walk this road once more. But as with all challenges we face, each experience also offers opportunity. It was during my second battle with breast cancer that a still small voice laid the idea to form a prayer group. Each Saturday morning a gathering of hope, healing, and holy community would lift to the heavens those fighting breast cancer, as well as their loved ones aiding the fight, and a plea for discovery that could end cancer's relentless grip.

That prompting blossomed into this anthology you now hold. Poetically crafted and spiritually reflective, these pieces offer a moving perspective on the emotional and physical journey of breast cancer diagnosis and treatment. Within these pages, you will find not only my story but also those of other courageous women recounting their struggles and triumphs through the lens of their faith. It contains the prayers offered and scriptures clung to for strength. This anthology aims to inspire and to let all impacted by this disease know that though the fight is difficult, through faith and fellowship there is light to be found, even in our darkest of days. We are all *Beautifully Crafted in God's Image.*

Prologue

In Acts 10:38 (KJV) it states, "How God anointed Jesus of Nazareth with the Holy Ghost and with power: who went about doing good and healing all that were oppressed of the devil; for God was with him." As we continue to lift breast cancer patients and their loved ones, know that God is with us and we are doing a good thing. He has anointed us to be an inspiration and beacon of hope in the lives of many. God has given us the Holy Spirit and the power to speak life and healing into the lives of many women struggling with breast cancer. They may never know our dedication, hear our prayers, or know our faithfulness to lifting them in prayer. However, we believe our prayers are moving on their behalf. God is with us and we firmly believe the prayers of the righteous are powerful and effective. We believe they are healed in the name of Jesus.

Stage 1 Why?

"My God! My god, why have you left me alone? Why is my help far away? I am crying out in great pain!"

Psalm 22:1 (EASY)

Why

Paralyzed at the sound of two words

Yearning, can this voice be unheard?

Frozen by this unpleasant emotion

Hoping not to give in to this notion

Fear is welling up inside

God, please give a quick reply

Why aren't you here

When you are needed the most

Drowning in fear

When you are not even close

Paralyzed by the sound of two words

Yearning, can this voice be unheard?

Frozen by this unpleasant revealing

Hoping not to give in to this feeling

Fear is welling up inside

God, please give a quick reply

Why aren't you here

Did you hear, it's breast cancer

Drowning in fear

Can you send a swift answer

A Mother's Dark Secret

You never mumble a word nor told a soul. You carried this dark secret all alone. This secret caused your body to deteriorate year after year, but you never mumbled a word nor told a soul. Never will I understand why you decided to walk this journey alone and not tell a single soul. But, within my heart, I believe you kept me safe from this burden because you believed this burden was yours and yours alone. Mother, please know you didn't have to bear this burden alone. My love for you would have dropped everything and helped you carry this load.

Mother, you never mumble a word nor told a soul. You carried this dark secret all alone. Did it ever cross your mind this secret would eventually be told? This dark secret was eventually told not by your words, but when your body could not take no more. For so long you carried this dark secret all alone, perhaps it was too late for medical intervention but not too late for you to share your load. I saw the relief in your eyes when we all helped you carry this burden you thought was yours alone. Mother, even though you withheld this dark secret until the very end; I let you go knowing you were never alone.

Oh, That Day

That day, oh that day

The day you went away

If only I had known

That day would be your last groan.

I moved on as life before

Not knowing what would be no more

If only I had known time was running out

I would not have left you without…

That day, oh that day brought regret, I do confess

I failed to see your deep distress

If only I had known

That day would be your last groan.

I will hold on to memories sweet

Of moments I love to repeat

That day, oh that day has come and gone

But your spirit will always live on.

Loss

When I first witnessed it, I was with you. But I did not understand the suffering that was behind her eyes. She was weak and she became weaker each day. The emotions she felt when she saw parts of herself wither away did not mean anything to me.

Why did she cry? In my defense I was young. Suffering was a small concept to me. Although I did not know the impact it would have on her, I said to her, "Don't worry, I still love you."

It was so long ago and the space between that day and the last day I spoke to her seemed only a minute long. On the last day we spoke, she gave me an assignment. Her wispy voice floated in the air. Like a heavy dream, I could not tell where it began or where it came from. But I obeyed.

I could not comprehend it then, but she had already left before she came to me. The times following that you comforted me. The moments I had then did not prepare me for now. And now that I am not with you it seems harder to bear.

These women were much closer to me. One yearned for life and one was ready. I did not know the difference in emotions that would leave with all those who love them. You see when they are ready, they leave us in such a peaceful place. We accept it much quicker. We understand it. We celebrate it.

When they are not ready there is this other feeling. Inner cold suffering. I do not blame them for not being ready. How could they be? They have so much more to give, so much more to offer. There is so much more they want to accomplish.

I could not imagine how it felt. They try to vocalize it in the best way they can. But I still cannot imagine it. I am sure you get these questions a lot. But why? Why can't we all get the same amount of time to prove ourselves to you?

Written by Naijah Cox

Just Thinking

Just sitting here thinking

When this cancer attacked my body

Just sitting here thinking

How it was messing with my mind

I will suffer and die

Just sitting here thinking

What effects it will have on my family

Just sitting here thinking

Those I thought would encourage me

They didn't

Just sitting here thinking

What a wonderful God we serve

You brought me through this sickness twice

Just sitting here thinking

How blessed I am to know and trust you God

Written by Alice Hamilton

You Were There

You were there when I first heard the news and no one in the room could comprehend the fear I felt. But you knew, so you held my hand and whispered everything would be all right.

You were there when I didn't understand the WHY and I felt you deserted me. Again, you still held my hand and whispered I'm not going anywhere, everything will be all right.

You were there when I felt the 'RED DEVIL' flowing through my veins. Yet, you were still holding my hand and whispering everything would be all right.

You were there when I cried as large chunks of hair fell to the floor and then there was no more. You still were there holding my hand and whispering you are beautiful, everything will be all right.

You were there when I went through the fatigue and all the discomfort and pain. You continued to hold my hand and whispered everything would be all right.

You were there when I went through the sad times that caused me to doubt you were there. Yet, you stayed there and never stopped holding my hand whispering everything will be alright. You were there LORD at every stage and LORD, you are still here.

Stage 2 Courage

"Have not I commanded thee? Be strong and of a good courage: be not afraid, neither be thou dismayed: for the LORD thy God is with thee withersoever thou goest."

Joshua 1:9 (KJV)

Courageous Sister

My sister, this is your daily reminder to be strong and courageous. Do not fret as this battle wages. Remember God has given you the ability to withstand things that scare others and cause others to throw in the towel. My sister, know that you are a fighter and HE has given you strength in the face of pain. HE has given you the ability to carry on despite the unknown. My sister, keep trusting in God for your source of strength. Even when you don't have all the answers continue to move forward in HIM. Faith is a choice and a willingness to confront agony and uncertainty in chaos. So, put your faith in the ONE who created you in HIS image. HE has you in the palm of HIS hands. Stay strong and courageous, my sister.

That Word

It scares us

It brings fear

It stays in our thoughts

We watch and hope and we pray

You are not here to stay

We believe in Christ our Savior

So, cancer you cannot and will not

Conquer our SPIRIT!

Written by Alice Hamilton

A Warrior's Courage

As this battle wages, draw courage from your heart

On this journey, a test of strength you start

Stand in sisterhood, stand as one in this fight

Walking in courage, helps your spirit take flight

Through the tears and pain, your spirit stays strong

With each step taken, intensifies your warrior's song

Burdens weigh heavy, yet your spirit's fire grows

Persevere sister, let your essence's brightness flow

It ignites with radiant light, that chases the darkness away

Though shadows come, on this path you will stay

With each treatment, stand shining your spirit's hue

Bravery looks beautiful when worn by a soul like you

Be encouraged and greet each day with steadfast grace

Face it with fortitude and never stop showing a warrior's

courage on your face

Stage 3 Hope

"We wait in hope for the LORD; he is our help and our shield."

Psalm 33:20 (NIV)

Hope

Hope flourishes within the fight

As we place our hope in Christ

Draw from HIS strength for this storm

Fierce warriors, we were born

Courageous hearts HE has made anew

HE is our help which will always be true

Now, gentle hands lifted up

HE will fill our empty cup

With support, love, and HIS healing touch

Hope whispers softly ever so much

Resilient souls find comfort in the Almighty

Hope is our guiding star from all anxiety

In the darkest of nights

Hope shines, a beacon of light

We shall win this fight

My Strength

My strength (I survived breast cancer)!

To stay strong when all is lost

I will shake off those harsh remarks

Whatever it cost

But I will remain strong

For there is hope

Stay strong for better days to come

Dark days won't last forever

There will always be the sun shining down

Staying strong to fight another day

Strength comes from experience, not education

Strength comes from pain, not pleasure

Strength comes from reason not emotion

Strength comes from being firm

Strength comes to conquer

Strength comes to survive

Most importantly my strength

Comes from God

Written by Alice Hamilton

Symbolism of Shades of Pink

The vibrant hues of pink evoke a great deal of emotions. From the soft pastels to the bold fuchsias, this spectrum represents youth, playfulness, and confidence. Yet, for some, certain shades take on a more somber meaning – the battle against breast cancer.

This formidable foe can leave a woman feeling drained, hopeless, and disconnected from her former self. The pain and challenges can be overwhelming, stripping away her strength and sense of womanhood. However, even in the darkest moments, the shades of pink serve as a reminder of the beauty, resilience, and hope within.

Like a radiant sunrise after a long night, these hues symbolize the promise of a better tomorrow. They remind us to draw strength from our faith, for God sees beauty in every woman, regardless of her circumstances. From the delicate blush tones to the rich, vibrant magentas, each shade of pink is a celebration of life, a testament to the indomitable spirit within every warrior battling this disease.

So, let us embrace the power of pink, for it is a beacon of hope, a rallying cry for those fighting, and a reminder that true beauty transcends physical form. In the face of adversity, let us find solace in these hues, and let them inspire us to stand together, united in our quest to overcome breast cancer, one shade of pink at a time.

Stage 4 Never Give Up

"I can do all these things because Christ makes me strong."

Philippians 4:13 (EASY)

Never Give Up

There is strength within the fight

Never surrender your light

The warrior within shines bright

Through trials and pain

Resilience gains

And courage reigns

As the battle rises up

The spirit remains untouched

Victory assured is the result

Never give up dear, stay true

Breast cancer cannot break you

Your heart's flame always burns through

Remember, you can do all things through

Christ who strengths you!

There is a CAN in Cancer

Within the word "cancer" lies an empowering message

"I CAN"

Cancer, you started this fight

CAN will finish this

CAN makes me stronger

CAN helps me face the challenges

CAN makes me brave

CAN teaches me not to give up

So, cancer has no place here

Inside of me lies a silent strength

I CAN SURVIVE

Written by Alice Hamilton

Still Able

You thought you brought me down

You thought you stole my crown

You thought I wouldn't dance

You thought I wouldn't have a chance

You thought I wouldn't chuckle or beam

But I am here to say it's all just a dream

Cancer in my breast couldn't keep me down

Surprise, I'm still able, prancing all around

I'm still able to do all with glee

Breast cancer you thought you won but see,

I'm still able and joyful as can be!

Gift of Now

Anger once ruled, but now gladness dwell

Hate staked its claim, but now loves to swell

Confusion flooded in, but now peace lies

Sadness grew, but now joy satisfies

Fear crept in, but now faith lifts its song

The pain took a grip, but now joy reigns all day long

Sickness flooded in, but now healing starts

Cherish the gift of now, that God did impart

God, offers more beyond what troubles you so

See life's beauty beyond what harms you know

This precious life, a treasure God crown

Never give up, continue to LIVE now

REMISSION

"LORD, please make me well again. Then I will be completely well. Rescue me so that I am completely safe. You are the one that I praise."

Jeremiah 17:14 (EASY)

Beautifully Crafted

This walk is a realm of strength and grace

A story of courage emerges to trace

Beautifully crafted in God's image are found

Warriors so brave we crown

With hearts so pure to face this fight

Through every challenge shine so bright

Spirits ascend like angels above

Embracing life with unyielding love

Each wound is a testament to the trials fought

Reminders of resilience, lessons taught

Stand together hand in hand

Rooted in a sisterhood forever stand

Beauty radiates deep within

A gentle reminder of the win

In this journey find the power

Converting pain into flourishing flowers

Like butterflies piercing from a cocoon

Rise above the darkness capturing the moon

Spirits ascend gracefully and free

A beacon of hope for all to see

Oh, beautifully crafted in God's design

Breast cancer warriors, oh how you shine

Your strength and courage an inspiration

A testament of love and determination

So, stand by their side, in support and care

With open hearts and a willingness to share

For in this journey, we shall find

The power of unity forever binds

Prayers

Dear God,

I come to you today with a heavy heart as my mother battles breast cancer. Please give me the strength and wisdom to support her through this trial. Grant me patience and compassion as I care for her, and help me lift her spirits with love and encouragement. Though the treatments are difficult to watch, I find comfort in knowing you are with us each step of the way. You are our refuge and hope in times of suffering. LORD, sustain my mother's faith and will to fight this disease. May the trials not overwhelm her but instead draw her closer to you. Give skill and insight to her doctors so they may provide the best possible care. And for myself, please quiet any fears or doubts, replacing them with peace. We cannot do this alone but find solace in your promise to never abandon your children. Thank you for hearing our prayers. We place full trust in your goodness, mercy, and plan for our lives. With you by our side, we will face each challenge with courage, strength, and faith that you will see us through.

In Jesus' name,

Amen

Dear God,

As I walk through this difficult time of facing breast cancer, I find comfort in knowing of your never-ending love for me. This illness brings physical and emotional pain, yet I take peace in remembering that you are always by my side. When I feel alone or afraid, I turn to you, the ultimate source of hope. Your Son, Jesus Christ, showed us the true meaning of sacrifice and unconditional love. Through his example, I am reminded that you love me fiercely, even in my deepest valleys. At each step of this journey, you carry me, and your love sustains me. You are my rock and my salvation. I pray that in the midst of whatever challenges come, I will continue feeling your presence, your comfort. You are always holding my hand.

In Jesus' name

Amen

Dear God,

I want to thank you from the bottom of my heart for your constant love and support. During the most difficult moments, when I received that devastating diagnosis, your peace was the only thing that got me through. Even though I was afraid, your Holy Spirit surrounded me with comfort. You gave me your Spirit as a companion, someone to lean on during life's hardest storms. Through it all, you have been by my side every step of the way. I know that you are always with me. Your faithfulness has given me the strength to make it this far. I am so grateful for your unending grace.

Thank you for walking with me, God. May your name be praised.

Amen

Dear Heavenly Father,

I come to you in your son Jesus' name. LORD, it was confirmed that I have breast cancer. LORD I am asking you to be with me on this journey. I don't know what to expect. I don't know what to do or who to talk to. LORD, please place the right people in my life to help me. I am afraid. Take this fear from me. LORD I am going to put all my trust in you. Lord, I know people will come and say negative things about this cancer, where to go, and what to do. LORD wherever you direct me that is my way. I heard bad things about chemo and what it can do to your body. You made us and you know our bodies. The surgeon and other doctors that are around me, give them wisdom on whatever needs to be done. LORD, I know you will be in control and I will be all right. I shall live!

In your son Jesus' name

Amen

Dear God,

As I face this challenge with breast cancer, I find comfort in knowing that you are sovereign over all things. You invite me to cast my fears and worries on you, for you can handle it all. Throughout my life you have proven faithful, you have never failed me, and have never let me down. In both good times and bad, you are always with me and always right on time. Today, I choose to place this burden in your hands. The fatigue, fear, hopelessness, and pain, it is all for you to take. You are my strength when I feel weak. You are my LORD and my God.

In Jesus' name

Amen

Dear Heavenly Father,

I come to you with gratitude in my heart for the many blessings in my life, even in times of struggle. Right now, I face a challenge with my health that feels overwhelming. The diagnosis of breast cancer has been difficult to accept. Yet I find comfort in knowing that I am not alone, you walk with me always. Your unending love and grace are my strength. When I feel weak, your presence sustains me. When I am afraid, your peace quiets my fears. I surrender this battle into your care, trusting that you have a purpose even in pain. Your word is truth, leave all my worries with you, for your burdens are light. This illness I cannot control, but I believe that you hold my future, and your plans for me are for good. So, I rest in your promises, that you will never fail nor forsake me. That all things work for good for those who love you. That greater is He who is in me than he who is in the world. This struggle will not defeat me, for you have already overcome. Thank you for walking with me, God. Thank you for your faithfulness. Be near to me each day, and help me find comfort and hope in you.

In Jesus' name

Amen

Dear LORD,

We ask with all hearts, to touch these special lives. Bless them with courage and hope, may they find comfort in your loving embrace. Heal them in their mind and spirit. Let their hope shine like a bright light that burns forever to honor their spirit fight. God cover them with the most precious blood of your son Jesus Christ, from the top of their head to the soles of their feet. Cast out anything that should not be in them. Destroy any unhealthy and abnormal cells in their body. LORD, you are our refuge, our fortress, our God, we put our trust in you. You are our healer, you have taught us that every act of healing is a miracle that comes from your unending grace. For we serve nothing but you who give us everything, because you are gracious and merciful. Bring life and healing to those breast cancer victims, fill them with your grace so that their bodies may heal and bring glory to you.

In Jesus' name

Amen

Heavenly Father,

I come before you today with gratitude for the gifts of life and health. For your ever-present protection and guidance, I am forever thankful. I lift (NAME) to you now, who is facing a challenge with their health. Being human, it's easy to feel fearful, but I know that you are sovereign over all things. You created this body with infinite wisdom and care. Father, I ask for your healing hand to bring renewed strength and wholeness. According to your perfect will and in your perfect time, remove all signs of illness from their system. Sustain them with resilience and hope as they undergo treatment. Surround (NAME) with circles of support. Fill their family, friends, and caregivers with compassion, empathy, and calm. Grant them reassurance of your love. Most of all, let your peace transcend all understanding and guard their heart and minds as they trust in you. You can do far more than we could ever ask or imagine.

We make this request through Christ our healer.

Amen

Dear God,

I want to express my gratitude for the success I've found. You made me with a spirit that cannot be overcome. As my creator in heaven, you are undefeatable. Being your child means the fight has already been won for me. Help me cling to the certainty of your teachings. Your scripture says you will stand by my side in battle against my opponents to secure my triumph. My adversary is breast cancer but I understand my Lord has guaranteed my victory.

In your son Jesus' name

Amen

Scriptures

Seeking God for healing

"LORD, please make me well again. Then I will be completely well. Rescue me so that I am completely safe. You are the one that I praise!"

Jeremiah 17:14 (EASY)

"Pray to me when you are in trouble. Then I will rescue you, and you will praise me."

Psalm 50:15 (EASY)

"Have mercy upon me, O LORD; for I am weak: O LORD, heal me; for my bones are vexed."

Psalm 6:2 (KJV)

"The LORD is a refuge for the oppressed, a stronghold in times of trouble. Those who know your name trust in you, for you LORD, have never forsaken those who seek you."

Psalm 9:9-10 (NIV)

Giving Praise for a healing

"I sought the LORD, and he heard me, and delivered me from all my fears."

>Psalm 34:4 (KJV)

"You have made me strong to fight battles, so that I win against my enemies."

>Psalm 18:39 (EASY)

"Praise the LORD, my soul; all my inmost being, praise his holy name. Praise the LORD, my soul, and forget not all his benefits – who forgives all your sins and heals all your diseases, who redeems your life from the pit and crowns you with love and compassion."

>Psalm 103:1-4 (NIV)

"For I am the LORD your God who takes hold of your right hand and says to you, Do not fear; I will help you."

>Isaiah 41:13 (NIV)

Strength and Comfort in God

"I can do all things through Christ which strengtheneth me."

Philippians 4:13 (KJV)

"Because God loves us, none of these troubles can ever beat us. He makes us win against them."

Romans 8:37 (EASY)

"May your unfailing love be my comfort, according to your promise to your servant."

Psalm 119:76 (NIV)

"God is our refuge and strength, an ever-present help in trouble."

Psalm 46:1 (NIV)

"Come to me, all you who are weary and burdened, and I will give you rest."

Matthew 11:28 (NIV)

"But they that wait upon the LORD shall renew their strength; they shall mount up with wings as eagles; they shall run, and not be weary; and they shall walk, and not faint."

Isaiah 40:31 (KJV)

Courage

"Have not I commanded thee: Be strong and of a good courage; be not afraid, neither be thou dismayed: for the LORD thy God is with thee whithersoever thou goest."

Joshua 1:9 (KJV)

"The Lord himself goes before you and will be with you; he will never leave you nor forsake you. Do not be afraid; do not be discouraged."

Deuteronomy 31:8 (NIV)

"I shall not die, but live, and declare the works of the LORD."

Psalm 118:17 (KJV)

Peace of God

"Do not worry about anything. Instead, pray to God about everything. Ask him to help you with the things that you need. And thank him for his help. If you do that, God will give you peace in your minds. That peace is so great that nobody can completely understand it. You will not worry or be afraid, because you belong to Christ Jesus."

Philippians 4:6-7 (EASY)

"Peace I leave with you; my peace I give you. I do not give to you as the world gives. Do not let your hearts be troubled and do not be afraid."

John 14:27 (NIV)

Hope in God

"We wait in hope for the LORD; he is our help and our shield."

                Psalm 33:20 (NIV)

"But those who hope in the LORD will renew their strength. They will soar on wings like eagles; they will run and not grow weary, they will walk and not be faint."

                Isaiah 40:31 (NIV)

Fear

"When you lie down to sleep, you will not be afraid. You will sleep well with peace in your mind. You will not be frightened of any trouble that might surprise you. Trouble may destroy wicked people, but you will know that you are safe. The LORD is the one who will take care of you. He will protect you, so that no danger can hurt you."

Proverbs 3:24-26 (EASY)

"Even though I walk through the darkest valley, I will fear no evil, for you are with me: your rod and your staff, they comfort me."

Psalm 23:4-5 (NIV)

Patience

"It is good when people continue to hope. It is good when they quietly wait for the LORD, because he will save them."

Lamentations 3:26 (EASY)

Worry

"Cast all your anxiety on him because he cares for you."

1 Peter 5:7 (NIV)

"LORD, you keep those people safe who continue to trust in you. You give them peace in their minds, because they believe in you."

Isaiah 26:3 (EASY)

Acknowledgments

I am deeply grateful as I reflect on the journey that brought us to this moment. First and foremost, I wish to express my sincere thanks to collaborators Alice Hamilton and Sophia Norris for bravely sharing their personal breast cancer experiences. Your willingness to be vulnerable provided the inspiration and foundation for this work.

Bishop Tanya Hanks, I am deeply grateful for you and all you bring. Your encouraging words lift my spirit and remind me that even in difficult times, there is hope. Your support means more than I can say - it reminds me that I do not walk alone. Thank you for your light, for sharing inspiration freely, and for enriching our lives with your presence.

I am forever indebted to my loving and generous husband, Petrece Robinson. Thank you for believing in my vision and supporting the creation of URDestined Publishing LLC. Your unfailing encouragement gave me the strength and courage to pursue my purpose.

To my beautiful daughter, Naijah Cox, you are my constant motivation. Thank you for the support and encouragement to step forward with courage and assurance each day. Your support inspires me to hold my head high. Your fire keeps me striving to be my best self.

To my wonderful and hilarious son, Cameron Cox, thank you for keeping me on my toes and reminding me to enjoy the little moments. Your playful spirit brings me such joy.

In enhancing this literature, I am grateful to Hypotenuse AI for generously providing their language expertise. This assistance was granted between the months of April and July 2024, which helped elevate the work.

I offer this book with a full heart, humbly hoping it may offer hope, healing, and empowerment to all who read it. My deepest thanks to each soul who played a role in bringing this labor of love to fruition.

About the Author

Ruby Robinson is an inspirational author, poet, and two-time breast cancer overcomer. Determined to share the lessons she learned from overcoming breast cancer twice, Ruby Robinson founded URDestined Publishing LLC to share inspirational literature that can uplift and motivate others. Her debut piece of literature, *Beautifully Crafted in God's Image*, shares Ruby's story of faith, hope, and healing through her breast cancer journeys. Ruby aims to inspire and empower other women facing health challenges and life's difficulties through her writing and speaking. She believes we are all destined for great things and *Beautifully Crafted in God's Image*.

Contribution by

Alice Hamilton is a quiet but passionate woman. Born in 1953 in Ocala, Florida, Alice is a two-time breast cancer survivor who devoted her life to sewing. She began sewing at the age of eight and spent her entire career working in sewing factories. Alice worked at her first sewing factory for 14 years before spending another 19 years at a second factory, rising to the position of assistant supervisor by the time she retired. In her time, Alice enjoyed sewing for weddings and events. She also loves to travel and her favorite vacation memory was taking a cruise that toured the Hawaiian Islands. Alice is known as a patient, caring woman who approaches life with joy despite facing challenges with her health. Sewing brought her immense fulfillment and she passed that passion on through her work and the items she created.

Sophia Norris is a remarkable woman of faith. A native of Florida, she has been married to Reuben Norris for over 45 years and they were blessed with three children. Tragically, two of their children passed away. Sophia has three grandchildren who bring her great joy. She worked for a car rental company for over 38 years. Sophia's life was transformed by two pivotal experiences – overcoming breast cancer twice and finding Jesus Christ as her Savior. She now sees herself as a witness for the Lord and believes that with God, all things are possible. Sophia enjoys sharing her story of how her Christian faith gave her strength to endure life's hardest trials and find meaning and purpose.

www.ingramcontent.com/pod-product-compliance
Lightning Source LLC
Chambersburg PA
CBHW060430050426
42449CB00009B/2227